SOUND WORDS

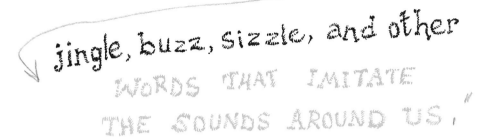

jingle, buzz, sizzle, and other WORDS THAT IMITATE THE SOUNDS AROUND US.

Published by
Lerner Publications Company
Minneapolis, Minnesota

[C1976]

International Standard Book Number: 0-8225-1109-6
Library of Congress Catalog Card Number: 76-22438

1 2 3 4 5 6 7 8 9 10 85 84 83 82 81 80 79 78 77 76

Sound words are called echoic (eh-KO-ick) words because they echo and imitate the natural sounds of objects, things, and actions. The word *buzz* echoes the sound made by a bee, just as *hiss* imitates the sound a snake makes. The use of echoic words—or "sound words"—in poetry is called **onomatopoeia** (AHN-uh-MAHT-uh-PEE-uh).

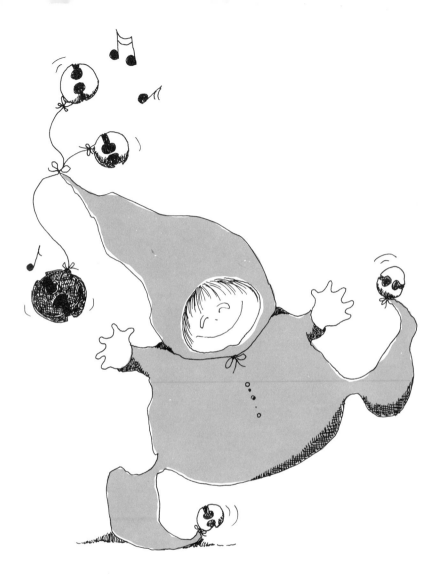

Jingle

Rattle

Crunch

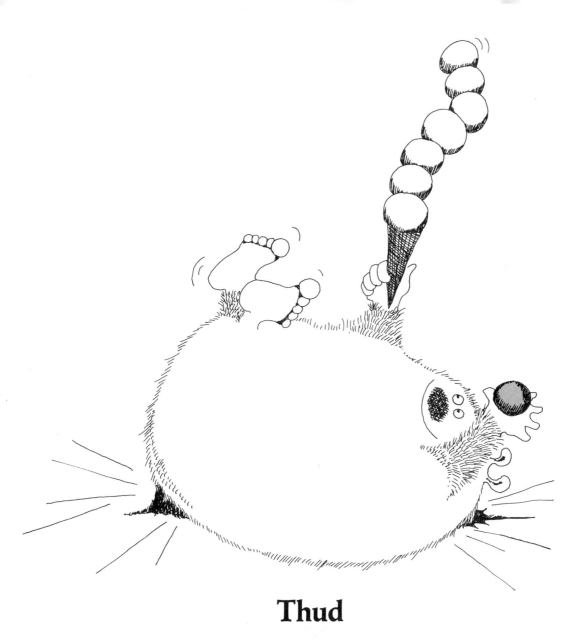

Thud

Fizz

Sizzle

Huff

Croak

Swat

Smack

Pop

Boom

Plop

Splash

Hoot

Tweet Chirp

Peep!

Slurp

Burp

Squawk

Snicker

Zip

Snip

Hiss

Buzz

Honk

Beep

*We specialize in producing quality books for
young people. For a complete list please write.*

LERNER PUBLICATIONS COMPANY
241 First Avenue North, Minneapolis, Minnesota 55401